PROPERTY OF
MOUNT AYR COMMUNITY SCHOOL

```
634         Goldman, Ethel
Gol
            I like fruit
```

	DATE DUE		
Truggs			
FEB			
NOV 8			
NOV 8			
FEB 10			
SEP 15			

MOUNT AYR COMMUNITY SCHOOL
ELEMENTARY LIBRARY

I LIKE FRUIT

By ETHEL GOLDMAN
Illustrated by SHARON LERNER

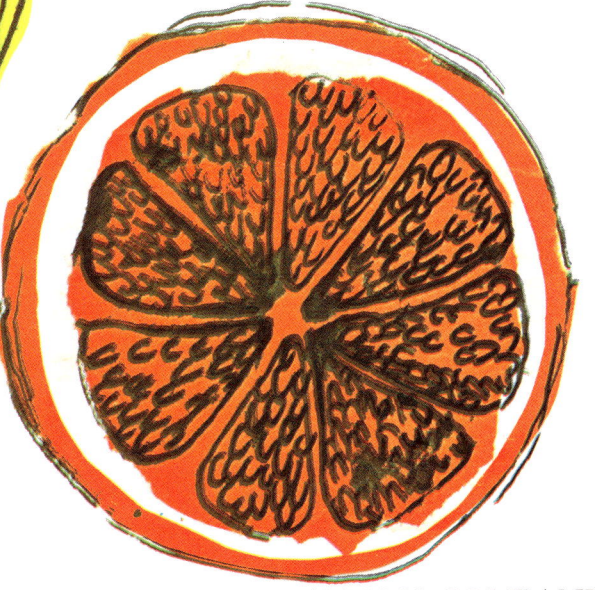

LERNER PUBLICATIONS COMPANY
MINNEAPOLIS, MINNESOTA

Copyright © 1969 by Lerner Publications Company

All rights reserved. International copyright secured. Manufactured in the United States of America. Published simultaneously in Canada by J. M. Dent & Sons, Ltd., Don Mills, Ontario.

International Standard Book Number: 0-8225-0270-4
Library of Congress Catalog Card Number: 68-56699

Second Printing 1971

CONTENTS

INTRODUCTION 5-7
ORANGES 8
STRAWBERRIES 10
BANANAS 12
APPLES 14
WATERMELON 16
PEACHES 18
PLUMS 20
PINEAPPLE 22
CHERRIES 24
PEARS 26
COCONUT 28
GRAPES 30

To my Family

I like fruit.
I like to bite into a crisp red apple.
I like to drink a glass of refreshing orange juice.
I like the taste of a just ripe banana.
I like a sweet watery slice of delicious watermelon.
I like to pluck a tart purple grape off a loaded stem.
I GUESS I LIKE TO EAT FRUIT, ANY FRUIT.

A fruit is the part of the plant which houses and protects the seeds.
Almost all plants bear fruit.
We eat fruits as vegetables.
Corn, tomatoes, and squash are fruits we eat as vegetables.
The fruit of some plants we eat as nuts.
Cloth is made from the fruit of the cotton plant.
In this book we will learn about fruits we commonly think of as "fruit."

Fruits are divided into four groups.
There are *core, stone, berry,* and *aggregate* fruits.
Each group has its own special seed arrangement.

Core fruits have several small seeds grouped together in the center around a core.
Apples and pears are core fruits.
Cut an apple in half and you can clearly see its core.
Peaches, plums, cherries, and apricots are stone fruits.
Stone fruits have one large hard seed in the center of their pulp.
Berry fruits have their seeds hidden throughout the fruit.
There are many different fruits in this group.
Some fruits you wouldn't expect to be are berries.
Watermelon, grapes, and bananas are berries.
So are citrus fruits, oranges and lemons.
Strawberries, blackberries, raspberries, and pineapples are aggregate fruits.
An aggregate fruit is made up of many tiny fruitlets each with a seed.

I LIKE ORANGES!
      A glass of orange juice gives the day a fine start.
      I like to peel the thick cushiony skin of an orange and eat its sections one by one.
      It is interesting to cut an orange in half.
      What a wonderful design the sections make!

Oranges are a citrus fruit.
Lemons, grapefruit, and limes are citrus fruits, too.
Citrus fruits are especially good for us.
Citrus fruits have thick, oily skins.
Their pulp is divided into many sections.
Each section contains one or more seeds.

Oranges and other citrus fruits grow best in warm climates.
Oranges are easily injured in winter frosts.
To protect the fruit on cold nights, orchard growers place oil heaters around their trees.
The warm smoke helps to keep the fruit from freezing.
Oranges grow well in California and Florida.
They are a very important crop in these states.
Each year the United States produces millions of tons of oranges.

There are many kinds of oranges.
The Valencia is sweet and very juicy.
The Navel orange is less juicy, has no seeds, and is very good for eating.
Mandarins are a Chinese orange.
They have an easy-to-peel skin.
Mandarins and tangerines are very much alike.

I LIKE STRAWBERRIES!
What a delicious idea, strawberry shortcake.

Strawberries grow on a short ground-hugging plant.
Runners go out in many directions from the mother plant.
Wherever they touch the ground these runners form roots.
In this way new plants begin to grow.

Strawberries have grown wild in Europe since very early times.
By the 15th century they had become a garden crop.
When the colonists arrived in America they discovered small wild strawberries growing everywhere.
From these wild strawberries the big, juicy red berries we enjoy were developed.
Today strawberries are grown in most of our 50 states.
The many little yellow or brown dots on the strawberry are its seeds.

Strawberries are eaten in many ways.
They make wonderful jam or jelly.
Strawberry ice cream and strawberry sundaes are old favorites.
Strawberries in cream are a breakfast treat.

I LIKE BANANAS!
>They are soft and mellow and nice to swallow.
>In a rain storm a big banana leaf would be a fine umbrella.

Bananas first grew in Asia.
They were brought here by a Spanish priest who wanted to win the friendship of the Indians.
This gift has become the main crop of many South and Central American countries.

Bananas grow on an interesting and unusual plant.
Each plant produces only one bunch of bananas.
Then it dies and is cut down.
From the old base a new stalk springs up.
In a few days this new stalk can be three feet high with several leaves and one small blossom.
This blossom grows into a bunch of bananas which can weigh 80 to 130 pounds and have over 100 bananas.
The banana bunch is divided into clusters called hands, and the bananas are called fingers.

As the bunch grows heavy, the stalk bends downward and the bananas hang with their points up.
A strange way to grow — upside down.

Bananas are usually picked and shipped green.
They are best eaten when they are just ripe.
A ripe banana is usually yellow, but there are red, pink, purple, and tan ones, too.
Bananas are most often eaten raw.

I LIKE APPLES!

    I like their rosy red cheeks.
    I like their beautiful pink and white blossoms that welcome spring.
    But best of all I like apple pie and applesauce.

Apples are probably the most popular of all fruit.
There are more apples eaten than any other kind of fruit.

The history of the apple goes back thousands of years.
Cavemen living in what is now Europe ate apples.
Remains of apple seeds have been found in their caves.
The American Indians ate sour wild apples.
The colonists brought seeds for sweeter apples to America.
Johnny Appleseed carried apple seeds throughout the Middle West.
Wherever he traveled apple orchards grew up.

There are over 1,000 different kinds of apples.
Here are a few: Wealthy, King David, McIntosh, Northern Spy, Yellow Newton, and Jonathan.
Each variety has its own special taste, color, shape, and use.
The Grimes Golden has a wonderful sweet and juicy taste.
Most crab apples are small and sour.
When you bite into a Baldwin it is yellow; the inside of a Rome Beauty is white.
The Rhode Island Greening has yellow skin and the Winesap a dark red skin.
The Delicious is just for eating while the Yellow Transparent is better for cooking.

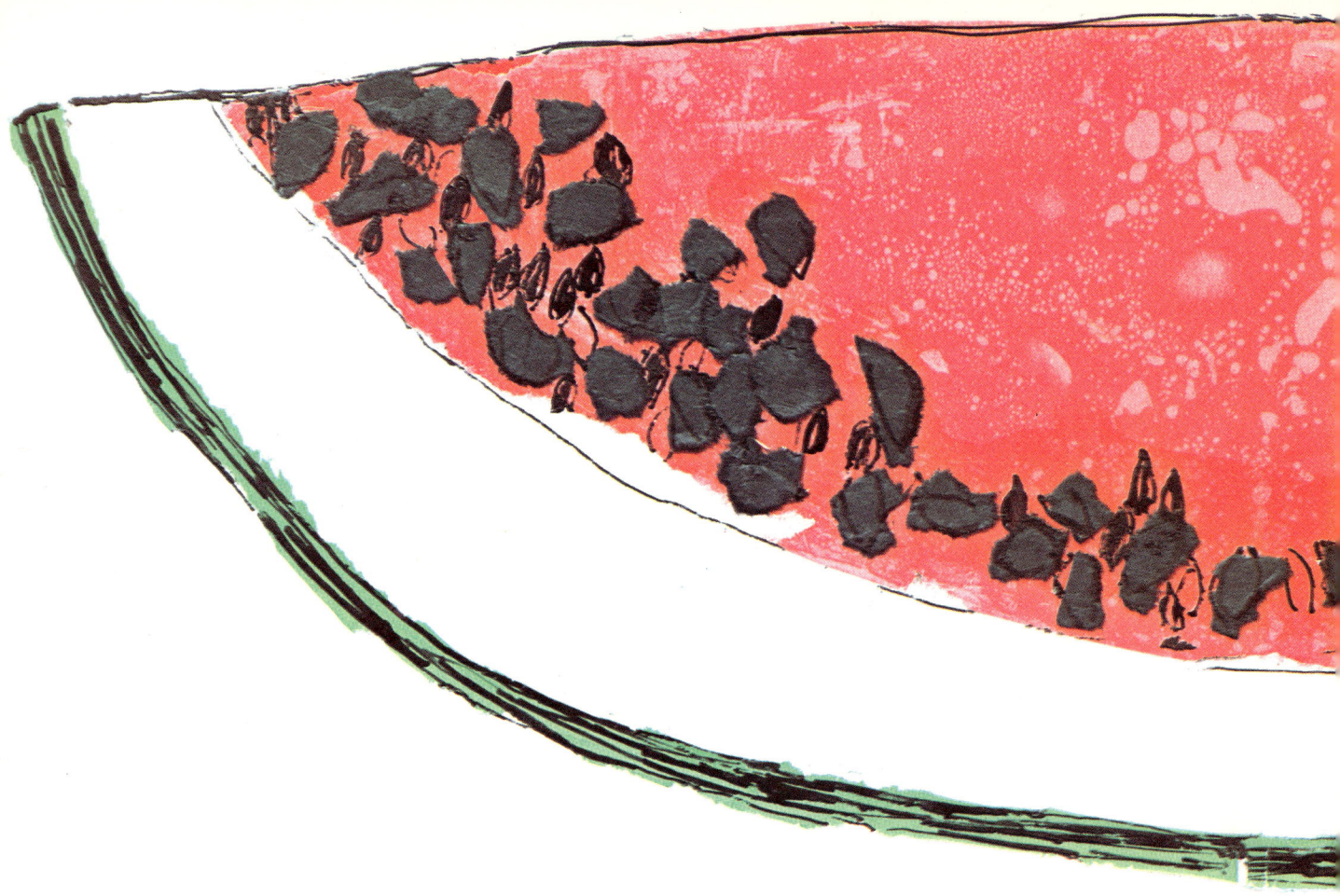

I LIKE WATERMELON!

Nothing tastes better on a hot summer day than a great piece of cold watermelon. A slice of watermelon with its many colors is a very pretty sight.

Watermelon is a large berry that grows on a low vine.

The watermelon plant lives and bears fruit for only one season.

It does best in a warm sunny climate.

Georgia, California, Texas, South Carolina, and Florida are our leading watermelon growing states.

Early African tribes first grew watermelons.
Later they were planted in Egypt.
Eventually the seeds were carried by merchants and travelers to Europe and Asia.
Watermelon seeds were probably brought to this country on slave ships.

Every bit of the watermelon is good to eat.
The rind makes fine pickles and preserves.
Some people enjoy the seeds roasted.

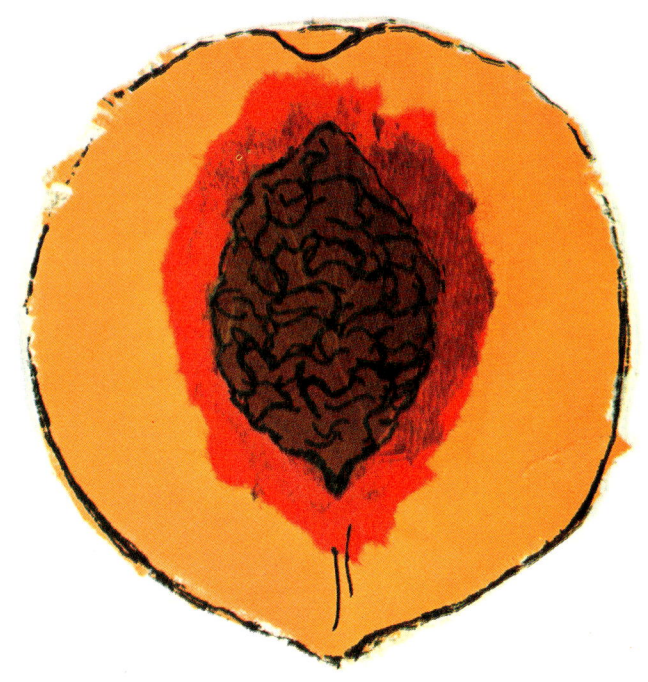

I LIKE PEACHES!
    I like to touch their fuzzy skins.

The peach is a stone fruit.
Its one seed has a hard covering.
Some peach stones cling tightly to the fleshy part of the peach.
These are clingstone peaches.
Others with loose-fitting stones are called freestones.
Freestone peaches are best for eating and clingstones are better for canning.

Peach trees can grow very tall.

Each year one tree can produce over a bushel of fruit.
Ripe peaches are rather soft and bruise easily.
They must be handled very carefully by the pickers.

Peaches were enjoyed by the Chinese over 4,000 years ago.
Travelers returning from China brought peaches westward to Europe.
The Spanish conquerors of Mexico introduced the Indians to peaches.
The United States is a major peach-growing country.

I LIKE PLUMS!
    I like prunes.
    Prunes are a special kind of dried plum.

The plum, like the peach, is a stone fruit.
Its stone can be either freestone or clingstone.
Its skin is always smooth.
There are many different kinds of plums.
The Italian and Greengage are wonderful eaten fresh.
Others like the Damson are sour and best cooked as jam or plum butter.
Plums can be small as a marble or big as an egg.
Their color can be dark blue, purple, red, green, or yellow.

People have eaten plums for thousands of years.
Pits of plums have been discovered with the remains of very early man.
The Damson plum gets its name from the ancient city of Damascus.
It grew there in large numbers.
The American Indian liked plums.
He found them growing almost everywhere.
Idaho, California, Oregon, and Washington have many plum orchards.

I LIKE PINEAPPLE!

It looks like a large pine cone.
The early Spanish explorers thought so too.
They called it *pina de los Indies* or "pine-cone of the Indies."

Most pineapples are grown in Hawaii and some in the West Indies.
They grow best in a warm place.
The pineapple is grown from a *cutting,* or a piece of stem which has been rooted.
Sometimes the crown or spike-leaved top of the pineapple plant is rooted and planted.
The pineapple plant grows to a height of about three feet.
One fruit grows on each plant.
It takes almost two years to grow one ripe pineapple.
They usually weigh from one to five pounds.
Record pineapples have weighed as much as 15 pounds.
Like the banana plant the pineapple plant dies when its fruit ripens.
New plants are grown for the next crop.

Pineapples have a tough prickly skin.
Under this skin is a juicy yellow fruit.
Pineapple is most delicious when it is fresh.
But often it is canned or frozen.
It can be bought sliced or crushed, in chunks or juice.
Pineapple topping is good on ice cream.
Pineapple juice is many people's favorite.

I LIKE CHERRIES!

Birds like cherries.
Birds have carried cherry seeds from place to place.
They carried cherry seeds great distances from Asia to Europe.
Many a cherry tree was planted by a bird.

Colonists brought cherry seeds across the sea to the New World.
Cherry trees didn't do well in the warm climate of Florida and the West Indies.
English settlers had good luck with them in cooler Massachusetts.
Hundreds of different kinds of cherries grow in the cool parts of the United States and the rest of the world.

There are two groups of cherries.
Sweet cherries are good for eating raw.
Sour or pie cherries are best for canning and cooking.
They make good cherry jam and cherry pie.

Cherries can be very dark red, black, bright red, or yellow.
All cherries are a small marble-sized fruit with one hard seed.
They are stone fruits related to the peach, plum, and apricot.

Some famous cherry trees line the boulevards and Capitol grounds in Washington, D.C.
They were given to the United States in 1909 by Japan as a token of friendship.

I LIKE PEARS!
> What a wonderful juicy flavor they have.
> You can always tell a pear by its special shape.

People have enjoyed the taste of pears for a long time.
In their wall paintings, early Egyptian artists pictured people eating pears.
The ancient Greeks celebrated a festival of pears.
The Romans grew many different kinds of pears.
The Sand pear was grown by the Chinese and Japanese for its beautiful blossoms.
The gritty, dry-tasting Sand pear wasn't good to eat.
Many of the pears we like today were developed in France during the 19th century.

There are many varieties of pears.
The Sechel pear is green and bronze in color.
It tastes sweet and spicy.
The yellow Bartlett pear is good for both eating and cooking.
The Bosc pear has a brown skin and crisp flavor.
The Anjou pear is green or yellow with rosy cheeks.
It is very juicy.

Pears grow best in mild weather.
Cold winters can hurt a pear tree.
California, Oregon, and Washington grow most of America's pears.

I LIKE COCONUT!
> But there is work to do before you can enjoy this fruit.
> Hit the hard shell with a hammer and watch the white liquid rush out.
> Then break the white meat from the shell.
> The taste of coconut is worth the work.

Coconuts grow on a tall slender palm tree.
These trees do well only in a tropical climate and usually near water.
They need little attention.
At the top of the tree are many fringed leaves.
Among these leaves in bunches of 15 to 20 grow the coconuts.
Coconut shells are hard and brown and have a hairy covering.

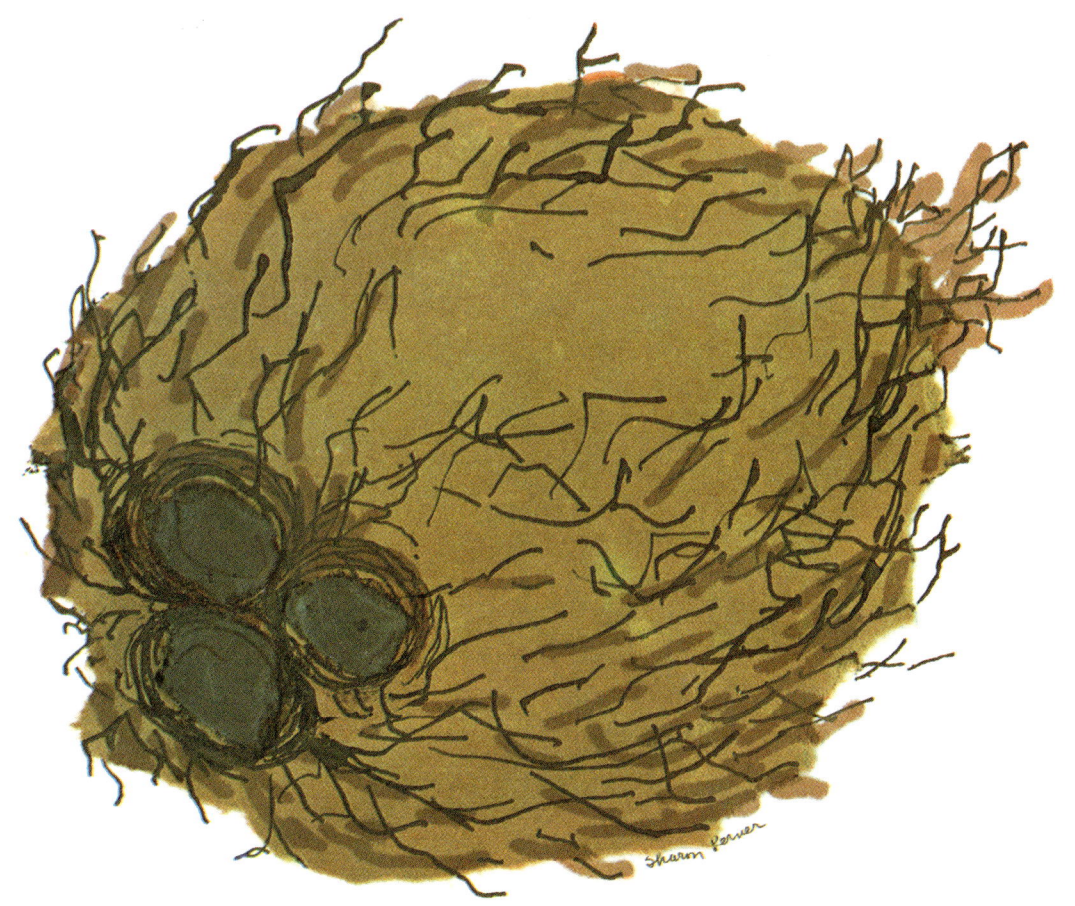

Inside the shell is a white liquid.
As the coconut ripens most of this liquid changes into firm white fruit.
A ripe coconut weighs between one and two pounds.

The coconut tree is one of the most useful plants.
Its trunk is used for wood.
The leaves are braided into hats, baskets, and cloth.
The hairy covering on the shell is very tough.
It is used for doormats, rope, and brushes.
The shell itself can be used as a drinking cup.
Coconut oil makes shampoo and cooking oil.

The fruit is delicious both fresh and dried.
Shredded coconut is a tasty part of many candies, pies, cakes, and cookies.

I LIKE GRAPES!
>It's fun to pluck a grape off the stem and pop it in your mouth.
>I like raisins, too.
>Raisins are dried grapes.

Grapes are berries.
Grape seeds are hidden in the center of the fruit.
Grapes grow on vines or shrubs.
These vines climb with the help of little curly stems called *tendrils*.
The tendrils reach out and wind around branches, wires, or whatever they can touch.
The place where grapes are grown is called a vineyard.
When the Vikings came to America, they found so many wild grapes growing they called this country Vinland.

The Bible often mentions grapes and wine.
Most wine is aged, or fermented, grape juice.
It is enjoyed the world over as a beverage.
Wine is used in many religious ceremonies, too.
Two fine wine grapes are Concord and Catawba.
California and New York are the largest grape-growing states.

Grapes come in many colors and have different shapes.
Concords are a small, deep purple grape.
Tokay grapes are oblong and reddish in color.
Thompson Seedless are small, olive-shaped, and light green.
Malagas are red or white and bigger and rounder than the Thompson Seedless.

ABOUT THE ARTIST AND AUTHOR

Mrs. Ethel Goldman is a graduate of the University of Minnesota. For the past fourteen years, she has taught fourth grade in the West St. Paul Public Schools. She has traveled extensively in the United States, Europe and the Middle East.

Mrs. Goldman has joined talents with her artist daughter, Sharon Lerner, in creating *I Like Fruit*. Sharon Lerner is a graduate in Art Education from the University of Minnesota, and has taught at University High School and Walker Art Center in Minneapolis, and the White Bear Public Schools. She has also illustrated a number of books for children.